COOL DOGS
COOL HOMES

COOL DOGS
COOL HOMES

living in style with your dog

GERALDINE JAMES

Photography by
JAMES GARDINER

CICO BOOKS
LONDON NEW YORK

Published in 2020 by CICO Books
An imprint of Ryland Peters & Small Ltd
20–21 Jockey's Fields
London WC1R 4BW
341 E 116th St
New York, NY 10029

www.rylandpeters.com

10 9 8 7 6 5 4 3 2 1

A CIP catalog record for this book is available from
the Library of Congress and the British Library.

ISBN: 978-1-78249-879-7

Printed in China

Editor: Carmel Edmonds
Designer: Toni Kay
Photographer: James Gardiner

Art director: Sally Powell
Head of production: Patricia Harrington
Publishing manager: Penny Craig
Publisher: Cindy Richards

with dogs before, but we found that there isn't much a dog won't do for a small piece of cheese or a treat. I have tried to show dogs in different environments and settings, but there was one thing they all had in common—access to all areas, with the home being as much the dog's as the owner's.

Eddie is a rescue dog, and so I also wanted to use this opportunity to expose the plight of many dogs globally; I hope that in some small way the efforts of selfless people and organizations are highlighted.

If we can make a difference to one dog's life, it will be worth it.

This project has been fascinating: visiting beautiful homes with all kinds of dogs has been inspiring and rewarding. Seeing dogs who have had a bad start in life now lying comfortably on the biggest bed or softest rug, or running through open fields and along the seashore, is especially uplifting. Watching how a dog can transform their owner's life, too, is something quite special.

URBAN DOGS

**EDDIE, DOUGIE, FLYNN, PEGGY, MONKEY AND MYRTLE,
WINNIE AND FLORA, BAILEY**

> "Eddie likes to stand guard at the window—he is well-known locally and passers-by are always photographing him."

EDDIE—CITY APARTMENT

OPPOSITE *Eddie eats in the kitchen. He has some extremely eccentric habits and likes the door to be open when he eats. My kitchen has dark gray floorboards which are very practical and don't show the mess, but the walls are all white. I'm forever changing the mixture of art and photographs on the walls.*

PAGE 12 *Large bay windows provide Eddie with a very good view of all the goings on in the street. I have covered the back of the couch with a cream linen throw and on top of that is a piece of African mud cloth, both picked up at a flea market. A sheepskin rug covers the arm to protect it against paw-marks.*

We have had Eddie since 2012, when we were lucky enough to adopt him from Battersea (the Dogs and Cats Home) in London. He is our second rescue dog, and although we don't know for sure what breed he is, we think he is a Parson Russell Terrier. We named him Eddie after the dog in the American TV show *Frasier*.

I have lived in this apartment in southwest London for many years. It's a spacious two-bedroomed home with a garden, which is ideal for Eddie, who spends most of his day patrolling both the front door and front bay windows and protecting us from the mailman, delivery men, and anyone else who approaches. Like all dogs he is fiercely loyal, and he is extremely devoted to me. He sleeps on my bed every night and really doesn't have a favorite spot in the apartment unless I'm there. He will sit at my feet wherever I am—in the kitchen or the office—or lie next to me on the couch. When I was working full time, Eddie had a dog walker who took him out on days that my

daughter couldn't have him. She lives nearby and still takes him for me when necessary.

My professional life in homewares buying has fed my passion for interiors, and it's important to me that my home is reflective of seasonal and current trends, but above all comfortable. I've collected both art and objects from years of flea-market buying and have some very treasured items which are valuable just in the sheer joy of owning them.

Most of the apartment has painted floorboards, which are easy to maintain. I've recently added some natural rugs for comfort and warmth, but I often come home and find them all over the place because Eddie has run to the front door or rushed around when he has heard a noise.

My style is quite mixed; I combine textures and prints, and I love walls of art and

RIGHT *On the white wall, a single painting bought in Pézenas, France is complemented by the tonal shades of the animal print blanket and black throw on the couch, which are soft and comfortable for both me and Eddie.*

photographs; I would say I'm on the maximalist spectrum. I like to have fresh flowers and candles burning, which create a warm and welcoming environment.

Owning a dog and keeping a lovely home is easy as long as you are not too set in your ways or concerned with keeping everything pristine. In the process of putting together this book I have found that however nice the home, the dog is very much part of the family and is included in almost everything that goes on, which generally means allowing access to all areas. Eddie and I live our lives together and I'm not worried about

The bed is probably the place you would most often find Eddie resting. Because my apartment is on one floor, he can see me from this spot if I'm in the living room or the office. A dark throw protects the bedcover from muddy marks.

getting paw marks on my cream linen sofas, I just have lots of throws on them that can be washed and changed as necessary. He is always in and out of the garden, so I have a towel ready at all times to wipe his feet when he comes in. I actually find humans are the messiest of all: spilt wine and food usually present more of a problem than the occasional muddy footprint.

The company of a dog also far outweighs any inconvenience or mess they bring with them—Eddie is the heartbeat of my home, and without him the cool interior would seem meaningless.

> " If I forget to close the bathroom door, Dougie would happily jump into the bath with me."

DOUGIE—TOWN HOUSE BY THE PARK

Dougie is a Red Lakeland Terrier and they are bred to be working dogs. He came from an arable farm just outside the city of Newcastle, in the northeast of England. Although eight years old, he has the energy and strength of a mature puppy who loves toys and games of tug. He is outgoing and very friendly, has twice-daily walks, and is always ready for his dinner. Like many dogs, he is motivated by food and treats. Unlike many dogs, Dougie also loves to be bathed and will happily jump into the bath with his owner given half a chance.

Dougie lives in Barnes, close to Richmond Park, one of London's iconic Royal parks, which is a perfect place for walking dogs. A stone's throw from central London and one of the UK's top sites for ancient trees, the park covers an area of 2,500 acres and has 630 red and fallow deer roaming freely within its boundaries. Dougie's owners, Marian and Richard, take him out regularly to enjoy the park and the other open spaces nearby. He also spends one day a week with a dog walker and he loves it; he is

OPPOSITE *These bespoke doors were commissioned when the owners bought the house back in 1993. A dog flap was installed when they first got Dougie as a puppy, giving him access to the outdoors all day. The house has a sunny south-facing garden, which Dougie loves.*

ABOVE *Beautiful arched doors open into a garden that Dougie can enjoy all day. Floorboards are painted dark gray throughout the kitchen, contrasting with a colorful rug beneath the long dark oak dining table. Leather modernist Danish dining chairs complete the room.*

very sociable and will happily go off for the day with his doggie chums.

In his mind, all the balls in the world belong to Dougie and he will capture any ball in sight and literally chew it to death—an expensive pastime, I'm told. He loves a fireside cuddle and brings his owners lots of happiness.

Dougie's home is a 1900s semi-detached house that was bought almost derelict in 1993. Gently restoring it over the years has been a labor of love,

Dougie sits on the squashy and very comfortable sofa covered in an Icelandic poppy-patterned fabric, which is very durable and easy to keep clean. Over the back is a Welsh blanket, and the sofa holds a combination of velvet cushions. The art above is plain gold leaf on an unframed canvas, a touch of warm color on a blue wall.

RIGHT *In the living room, there's a beautiful marble fireplace surround, found and installed by the owners. Floorboards are sanded and stained dark walnut, and what would have been two rooms is now one, allowing you to see straight through to the back of the house. An armchair covered in pale blue velvet provides another cozy spot for Dougie to rest in.*

OPPOSITE *This extension into the roof space was added several years after the original restoration, to provide a large utility space for doing the laundry and storing extra clothes and linen. The eaves windows provide the perfect space not only for Marian to sit and read but for Dougie to soak up the sunshine.*

which involved finding quality craftsmen to install bespoke doors, replacing fire surrounds, and extending into the attic. Dougie is pretty much allowed access to all areas of the house, and has his own dog flap so he can go outside whenever he wants. The wooden floors and rugs and their individual style make for an extremely comfortable home for both Dougie and his owners.

The decorating style is individual and his owner happily mixes colors and materials side by side over the house's three floors. Dougie explores them all, going wherever the company is, and loves nothing more than sitting on the chair under the eaves in the attic, with the warmth of the sun filtering in.

> " What Flynn lacks in stature, he makes up for in personality. "

FLYNN—CONTEMPORARY YET CLASSIC

OPPOSITE *This large open-plan kitchen space features a skylight that floods light onto the herringbone parquet floor. The "wow" tryptic prints are provided by John Patrick Reynolds who works with comic art and hang alongside an illuminated red theatrical number. In the foreground are a Saarinen dining table and chair.*

PAGES 26–27 *This space lies between the sitting room and kitchen and provides a cozy den for watching television and reading. The large leather buttoned ottoman, for putting your feet up or for a tray of food, is one of Flynn's favorite spots for keeping an eye on goings on.*

Little Flynn, a Maltipoo, is six years old and was rehomed from the dog rescue charity All Dogs Matter—read more about his story on page 160. He is an integral part of the home—like all dogs, he loves his routine, treats, belly rubs, chasing squirrels, and snoozing on the bed.

His owners, Andrew, Mark, and their daughter, Alicia, live in this beautiful large house in the southwest London borough of Wandsworth. As well as having great transport links to the city center, it is surrounded by parks, woodland, and the large space of Wandsworth Common, so is an ideal place to own a dog.

Full of confidence, Flynn has the nickname "Fearless Flynn"—he is king of the Common and not fazed by any other dogs, regardless of size. He loves to protect the garden from intruding birds or squirrels, even when they are not there, as he thinks it will earn him a treat. He knows when he is being taken to the dog grooming salon or vet and refuses to move, so he has to be carried—he is a very stubborn little man.

OPPOSITE *Three steps lead up from the den into the living room, which has white bay windows looking out onto the street. An original fire surround with a slate hearth has been restored during the renovation work. The steps offer another place for Flynn to watch proceedings.*

ABOVE LEFT *The urban glamour of old Hollywood is reflected in these black and white pictures. A pop of color in the pillow acts as a unique contrast to the blue-green walls.*

ABOVE RIGHT *It was a very hot day when we took these pictures, so Flynn took refuge on the cool slate hearth for some respite. He sits alongside an old statue bought in Sri Lanka.*

Mark and Andrew moved over eight years ago into the Victorian end-of-terrace house, which is in a smart residential area known as Nightingale Triangle. The name came after the area was recognized for its plush residential properties between Nightingale Lane, Balham, and Clapham Common. It has a reputation of having a small village-like feel, and its residents have regular community events and street parties.

The house has undergone modernization and renovation throughout the time Mark and Andrew have been there—it now flows well and has a bright, modern feel. The decoration style is extremely urban chic, featuring some surprising decorating ideas and lots of character—for example, the wonderful black and white photography, which gives a real Hollywood feel, and the giant "wow" prints in the kitchen.

Andrew and Mark enjoy the arts, theater, and contemporary design and this is reflected in their home. They are very adventurous with

LEFT *Reflected in the large industrial mirror hanging on the landing we see Flynn as he sits on the third floor. A small console table outside the master bedroom houses a quirky red table lamp, adding drama to an otherwise quiet corner.*

OPPOSITE *You will often find Flynn in the master bedroom, which is one of his favorite places; just like many other dogs, he prefers not to be too far from his owners. The single color walls and shelves are home to many treasured items— photographs of friends, a favorite David Bowie album cover, toys, and pieces of art—giving it a very personal feel.*

color and happy to mix the unexpected together. The house and garden are very well appointed as a party environment and Andrew and Mark host guests regularly. While it is very high spec, it is not uptight; they have created both cozy areas for watching TV and wide, open spaces for entertainment and dining. Piles of design books reflect their love of art, and family photographs add a homely feel.

There are four floors, with Alicia's haven on the top floor, an office space, and plenty of room for guests. All rooms have an individual decorative style, but work together to reflect the home's modern and colorful feel.

Flynn is a lucky dog to have found such a wonderful home with this family; it has certainly given him the confidence to develop his personality.

> " Every morning we try to take Peggy out after breakfast, but she ignores this and runs upstairs to sleep on our bed. "

PEGGY—ECLECTIC MIDCENTURY MODERN

Peggy is a seven-year-old Lurcher, a breed which is typically a cross between a Sighthound and a Terrier. Her owners, Ella and Magnus, found Peggy at Lurcher SOS—read more about her story on page 162. Lurchers are becoming popular as pets as they are very laid-back and, like Peggy, prefer a warm bed to anything else. However, they do like to chase, as is their reputation, and Peggy will go after a squirrel if she gets half a chance.

Ella owns a shop called A New Tribe in Hackney in east London, and Peggy goes there with her most days. When Peggy is not in the shop, she goes to a local dog walker, Tails and Shells. This gives her the chance to socialize with other dogs and get stimulation and exercise—it's a fun day for her away from the shop. If Ella and Magnus go away, Peggy has no shortage of weekend minders, including their friend Stephen among others—it sounds as if she has quite a following. For a longer trip or vacation, she goes to Nottingham to stay with Ella's mother.

OPPOSITE *The entrance is very cleverly contained by a glass paneled wall allowing light to enter the lounge through the unique stained glass. Peggy prefers lying on a rug—she doesn't like hard surfaces.*

Ella and Magnus moved into their 100-year-old three-bedroom terraced row house in Walthamstow two years ago. Walthamstow is a major district in northeast London, which has become more popular over the last decade as part of the city's suburban growth. The area has seen an increase in creative and artistic families and businesses, making it very sought after.

The house has a roof extension and a kitchen addition at the back. At the back of the house there is a train line, but thanks to the fairly long garden it's hardly visible. Magnus and Ella completely

gutted the property; it was in a very sad state and all the original features had already been removed, so they didn't feel bad about knocking everything down. When they first moved in, the bathroom was in the middle of the ground floor and it still had the original outside window. The renovation has been a labor of love and the overall effect is truly stunning; the attention to detail is remarkable and everything is well considered, extremely unique, and quite unexpected. I left the house feeling very inspired.

The style is quite eclectic, and Ella and Magnus like to mix designer classics, such as Vitsoe shelving and a vintage Bachelor chair by Verner Panton, with pieces they love. They have many of their own designs, originally sourced for the shop, and items collected on travels to Morocco when buying for the store. Magnus is a product designer and this has played a useful part in finding bespoke light fittings and furniture during the restoration process. Peggy particularly loves the sofas: the Tepee sofa is by SCP designer Lucy Kurrein, and the mud cloth

ABOVE *The Vitsœ shelving unit—designed in 1960 and still being manufactured today—can be customized as required and is available in many colors. In the foreground is another rug from A New Tribe and a bespoke pouf.*

OPPOSITE *Ella works at the dining table and so, as always, Peggy is not far away, languidly lying on yet another rug from Ella's shop in front of a stripped vintage medicine cabinet. The strong blue wall, coupled with the plants and pots, gives the effect of making you feel as if you were in Morocco.*

In the master bedroom at the front of the house hangs the most splendid raffia lampshade, a very dramatic statement in a room that has soft tones and eclectic art pieces.

ABOVE *In every room in the house, Peggy has a favorite space to lie down. This spare room at the back of the house features soft and comfortable bed linen. Looking through onto the landing, a cotton blanket entitled Parallel Movements by Californian art brand BFGF hangs on the wall.*

RIGHT *A New Tribe is Ella's shop, where Peggy has a legion of admirers and spends much time lying on the rugs, waiting for the next customer to give her a tummy rub.*

sofa is upholstered with fabric that was bought in Morocco.

The house is a masterstroke of unique design—what was a sad, unloved, almost derelict cottage is now eclectic midcentury modern with an underpinning of North African culture. The color combinations are unusual and unexpected but so clever that you can't fail to be inspired and encouraged to mix together different styles yourself. Peggy is the perfect pet to have in this home—like everything around her, she is beautiful and unique.

"I have a thing about names beginning with M, but Myrtle I call 'Wyrtle,'—bonkers, I know."

MONKEY AND MYRTLE— LUSH AND DRAMATIC TOWN HOUSE

OPPOSITE *In this very glamorous room, Monkey sits among items that can be bought at Abigail's store mixed with vintage finds, plants, and faux foliage. The dark walls and fire surround add drama, while the convex mirror reflects the stunning chandelier.*

Abigail Ahern and her husband Graham lost their beloved Welsh terrier, Maud, last year. Their other dog, Monkey, who is a super laidback, almost horizontal, terrier, started to retreat into himself and was anxiously chewing himself to the bone, just as when he was first adopted (read more about his story on page 164), so they took themselves to a farm in Wales and found Myrtle. Myrtle's mother generally spends the days whizzing over the hills rabbiting; apparently, she disappeared for a few days and came back pregnant. The rest, as they say, is history, as now Monkey and Myrtle spend all day playing, something Monkey and Maud never did.

Both dogs accompany Abigail to work but don't stay all day, as Graham mainly works from home, so they can have the run of the house and garden. They are walked twice a day at the nearby London Fields park—Graham does the morning and Abigail the evening—and they have a bunch of friends they meet and play with. At the weekend they are taken further afield, sometimes to Hyde Park in the city center to watch the sun come up as they are early birds. If not Hyde

Park, it could be Epping Forest on the outskirts of London, or Victoria Park in east London, where they walk along the canal to the local farmer's market. From time to time on Saturdays they all wander over to Borough Market and drink coffee, pounding the pavements and enjoying what London has to offer.

Abigail and Graham have lived in their house for twenty years. It's a very imposing 1860s town house with four floors and is in Hackney, a borough in inner east London. Most of the original workers' cottages and homes there are being gentrified and have become highly sought after; it is considered a very trendy area and attracts people in the creative world.

When they moved in, the house was in a state of total disrepair, so they ripped out the back wall over two floors and installed a wall of glass. They are still constantly renovating, updating, and decorating. Since Abigail has a design store and business, she

ABOVE *The colors and textures on the small sofa almost make Monkey disappear in this space. The huge double-height Crittall windows let light flood into the room, where there are warm tones, exposed brick, and lots of soft, cozy textiles and rugs.*

RIGHT & OPPOSITE *Myrtle has lost or found something interesting under the sofa. She treats the home as her own personal playground, jumping, diving, running, and tumbling with Monkey. The double-height windows and exposing the two floors makes this space feel like a loft apartment and allows for huge-scale art and mirrors.*

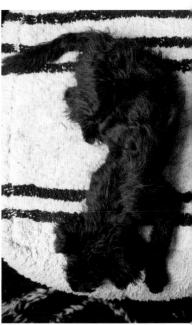

OPPOSITE & ABOVE *Monkey and Myrtle blend into their surroundings: Monkey sits on the shaggy sheepskin rug, while Myrtle leaps from the black and white pouf. The view of the verdant garden and the equally lush display indoors give the space the look and feel of an exotic climate.*

PAGE 46 *The master bedroom at the front of the house on a sunny day. Light streams in and the pop of turquoise adds glamour. Good blackout curtains and lots of pillows create a cocoon effect and a cozy sleep environment.*

PAGE 47 *In this room on the first floor at the front of the house, Myrtle matches the cowhide chair and indeed the whole room. The genius design trick of a mirror reflecting a chandelier is used again: it creates dimension and a sense of space. Warmth is added by both the foliage, which breaks up hard edges, and the soft textiles.*

runs monthly design workshops from her home each month for around 20 people at a time, which includes a tour of the house.

Abigail and Graham also completely re-landscaped the front and back gardens to look and feel like a jungle. A huge fig tree in the front garden offers a pleasing view, and they have planted other trees—eucalytpus, bay, and olive—with a wall of black bamboo to encourage them to grow tall and eventually provide privacy all the way up to the fourth floor. Abigail feeds them seaweed to help them grow.

Abigail's eponymously named store sells furniture, accessories, and faux flowers among other things. She travels extensively to India and China for her work and misses the dogs terribly. Her style is very bold and glamorous: she loves mixing dark colors and fabrics together. Her home is filled with lots of lush plants, layers of rugs on the floor, and multiple pieces of art on the walls, especially portraits. She works with her sister on the floral and foliage side of the business to create some pretty realistic and extraordinary plants and stems, which are seen in all the rooms in her house.

She has published many books on her style and color vision and is recognized widely as a design guru; she breaks down boundaries and has an extremely eclectic and brave approach to interior design.

> "Winnie is a big hugger and Flora is fiercely independent, but they are both highly motivated by food."

WINNIE AND FLORA— CONVERTED COACH HOUSE

OPPOSITE *Flora surveys her surroundings in the light, airy dining room, featuring copper lamps by Tom Dixon, a painting by artist Yvonne Coomber, and a very long bespoke dining table with a metal frame.*

Winnie and Flora live with Patrick and Sheila in north London. Winnie is a Labradoodle and was born in February 2009. Her mother was a black Labrador and her father a cream miniature Poodle, and she came from breeders in Mansfield, a market town in Nottinghamshire in the midlands of England. She loves swimming, chasing and retrieving balls, and playing tug with Flora. A very affectionate dog, she will stand on her hind legs and wrap herself around you. She often sleeps on her back with a toy in her mouth, hoping someone will pass by and give her a tummy rub. She was named after Patrick's mother's carer, who was delighted with her namesake.

Flora is a West Highland Terrier, born in May 2010. She came from a goat farm in Hertfordshire called Wobbly Bottom Farm, and does indeed have a wobbly bottom. She and Winnie are fed twice a day and Flora always quivers with excitement as soon as she hears the food drawer being opened. She was named by Sheila's mother after Flora McDonald, a famously strong, brave Scot, and

The dominant feature in the living room is the Tom Dixon Melt lamp in copper. The warm tones of the pillows contribute to a cozy, comfortable room. Flora is desperate to jump on the sofa!

ABOVE LEFT *This view from the front door shows Flora on guard duty in the hall and behind her the garden: raised beds with matching wood fencing and planted trees create a clean and modern appearance.*

ABOVE RIGHT *Looking back toward the front door, just out of sight, is the original stained glass from the coach house. On this beautiful sunny day we can see how light the house is, and the sun creates the perfect spot for Flora and Winnie to relax.*

lives up to her namesake. Fiercely independent, she does everything on her own terms and always with massive enthusiasm; she is a huge explorer and loves to discover new territory. However, she gets lost in her own world and often fails to come when called. Sheila's mother loved Flora and often asked if she was behaving herself; mostly the answer was no, which made her smile. When relaxing, Flora likes to sit near a human, preferably on the sofa.

Sheila and Patrick's house, which is in Kilburn in north London, was originally a Victorian coach house. In 2010 the land next door was put up for sale, so they bought it and a few years later hired an architect to create a modern, light, airy home with a double-height extension. Sheila and Patrick moved out while the work was being done and returned when it was finished in early 2015. They are thrilled with the result, which is a new home but one that retains some old features and provides extra space inside and out. It is a house that is filled with light.

> "Although he lives in an urban environment, Bailey behaves as if he lives in the country."

BAILEY—LIGHT AND MODERN HOME

OPPOSITE *At the back of the house is Penny's office space. Bailey sits in his bed, staring at the garden and trying to spot the cat or birds. The large picture window gives the room a bright, modern feel. This theme continues in the rest of Penny's home, which has been modernized throughout while retaining many original features.*

Bailey is a Cockapoo, though he thinks he's a working Spaniel like his mother. The intelligent Poodle gene from his father hasn't manifested itself yet and he's 18 months old. He lives in Chelsea in southwest London with Penny.

Loyal, fun, cuddly, good-natured, and bonkers in equal measure, Bailey is greatly loved by Penny's grandchildren, and he will play with them for hours without ever getting tired or bored. His routine in the morning is to run around the small patio garden three times, stopping to bark at the birds and the neighbor's cat if he's in sight, and then he's ready for breakfast. He has many friends among the local community whom he likes to run around with at the park.

Bailey's home is a four-story Victorian house. It was built in 1840 on a site previously owned by Sir Thomas More, a chancellor to King Henry VIII. Bailey likes to visit the statue of More in front of Chelsea Old Church. However, he is blissfully unaware of his historical surroundings and would prefer to live in the country. He seems to think nearby Battersea Park is the estate in Hampshire where he was born.

COUNTRY DOGS

ALFIE, BLIN, BONNIE AND BESS, SMITH, RONNIE,
RITA, RUBY, AND LENNY, COCO

"Alfie is extremely sociable, contrary, inquisitive, affectionate, competitive, and cantankerous in equal measure. However, he slotted into the family from day one."

ALFIE—GEORGIAN FARMHOUSE

OPPOSITE *The kitchen is the heartbeat of the house—and what dog doesn't like to be in close proximity to an Aga? This is definitely where the action and food are. The open door leads to the utility room, and the back door to the garden.*

Alfie is a Wire Fox Terrier, born in Iowa, US, in 2005 to one of the few Fox Terrier breeders in the US, and has led a very interesting and varied life. After a journey of a thousand miles, he arrived at his new home, a super-cool loft apartment in Soho in New York where he lived with Rick, Deb, and their two daughters, Molly and Darcy. He was a happy addition to the family and soon become top dog; he has a huge personality and an attractive disposition, and was something of a novelty in the city. His life was spent pounding the pavements and meeting other dogs at local dog spaces. If Rick and Deb needed a walker or kennels, he went to Happy Paws.

After a while, the family moved to Brooklyn, and suddenly park life became the norm. Their local park in Fort Green gave Alfie the chance to easily meet other dogs—as well as squirrels—and with the addition of a garden, life was pretty good for him.

In 2013, Rick and Deb decided to move back to the family farm in Kent, England. The contrast in his early days to the life he now enjoys is huge. The farm is surrounded by sheep and orchards, with rabbits galore. He is perfectly happy, spending his retirement with family, friends, and lots of animals. Although he is now 16, slightly hard of hearing, and doesn't vocalize as much as he used to, Alfie can still behave like a puppy and certainly doesn't look like an ancient dog.

The farmhouse that the family have owned since 1994 (and rented out while they lived in the US) was built in 1790. It is a typical flat-fronted Georgian farmhouse, and although it was once a dairy farm, it was also known for its orchards and prize-winning plums.

OPPOSITE *Alfie sits on the George Smith velvet sofa, which was in Manhattan and Brooklyn before it found its way to Kent. The large painting hanging over the midcentury marble-top credenza is by Marlene Dumas.*

RIGHT *On the opposite side of the living room, which was originally the dairy, are doors that open into the garden. Alfie sits in his new sheepskin-lined bed, looking full of anticipation.*

OPPOSITE *Upstairs in the master bedroom, Alfie likes to be part of the action. The cream-painted shutters, designed to replicate the originals, have been folded back to let the sun stream in.*

ABOVE LEFT *This balcony is positioned over the stairs and it makes an ideal spot for Alfie's observations. Beneath it you can see the curved glazed windows of the front door.*

With so many sheep in the surrounding fields, lambing season is a busy time, and one could almost mistake Alfie for a lamb—his soft, cream, curly coat makes him blend in with the locals.

The home is beautifully light and decorated with some of the furniture they had in the US. The kitchen features a classic Aga oven and has recently been renovated after suffering bad water damage. Rick and Deb continue to work on the garden and house since returning to the UK, and Alfie is always involved in all that goes on.

ABOVE RIGHT *The spacious garden is a wonderful playground for Alfie. A large pine tree shadows the al fresco eating space and outdoor kitchen. Beyond are the fields of grazing sheep.*

> "If I shout 'squirrels,' it gets him out of bed for a run around in the garden, otherwise he stays there as long as he can."

BLIN—REMODELED BARN HOUSE

Blin was born in Maidstone in Kent in August 2009 and is a standard Poodle. His Poodle pedigree name is Myall and his parents and grandparents are all Crufts winners, Crufts being the internationally recognized annual dog show. He was the last puppy in a litter of seven.

He lives with Jane, who is a garden designer, in West Grinstead, a village in West Sussex. The river Adur flows through the village and it is positioned between the South Downs range of hills and the English south coast beaches of Brighton, Hove, Shoreham, and Worthing. Around 50 miles away from London, it's a very desirable country home with easy access to all that the city offers.

Now that he is a bit older, Blin usually tries to stay on Jane's bed for as long as possible in the mornings. Once he is up, they wander around the garden and pond and feed the chickens, followed by a half-hour's walk, often in the neighboring fields and woodlands—they have many routes. Jane also drives to some of the beautiful forests and beaches nearby. From time to time they meet up with friends and

OPPOSITE *The oval Eero Saarinen dining table sits in front of the double-height windows, which show the stunning garden view and allow light to flood into the barn.*

wander over the South Downs
for a play with a pair of Cavapoos.

They walk again in the evening,
quite late in the summer and
just before dark in the winter.
The weather doesn't stop them,
but mud is a huge problem with
Poodle coats, meaning lots of
hosing down and brushing are
needed. Blin has a weekly bath
and a thorough brushing, which
he hates—Jane has to put him
up on the table so she can reach
all parts of his coat.

After the evening walk, Blin has
raw chicken for his dinner and he
and Jane settle for an evening of
television, or Scrabble for Jane
and savaging a toy for Blin. If Jane
has friends over, he usually goes
to bed as a protest for not having
Jane to himself. He is never far
from Jane's side; when she is
gardening, he sits in a bed of
grasses for comfort and keeps
close. If they're inside he sits on
the end of the sofa, which tends
to be his bed of choice.

Blin is a very chilled-out dog.
Although on an initial meeting
with someone new he is very
boisterous, he just likes to greet
them; it is a real Poodle trait. He
was a very willful pup and training

A huge open-plan living and dining space, with exposed wood beams at the kitchen end. Blin is in his favorite place at the end of the sofa. The painting of a black dress on a yellow background by Richard Nott adds a splash of color.

ABOVE *The snug room, formerly a stable, is a bright, colorful space for reading. The shelves are filled with Jane's collections of glass and the walls are adorned with art and precious family photographs.*

OPPOSITE *Blin walks across the landing that joins one bedroom to the other. One can get a real sense of the scale of the barn from the exposed beamed vaulted ceiling. Richard Nott's painting is seen more clearly from this aspect.*

seemed unachievable, but he behaves well now. He loves rough and tumble play with Jane and any dog who is up for it. Like most dogs, he loves chasing small creatures but rarely catches them; however, he hates swimming and puddles, which is strange as Poodles are water dogs.

The house, known as the Black Barn, was built in the 18th century and Jane moved in nearly two years ago. It was initially renovated in the 1970s, then remodeled in the 1990s when the tree house was built. It was originally a hay barn and in the 1970s housed lots of raves by the local kids. There were also stables and a tack room, which are now a snug room and an annex.

The beautiful garden covers two acres. It was not a flower garden initially, instead having shrubs and a long hedgerow right down the middle of the plot. Jane, being a garden designer, made changes: the hedgerow was replanted by the road, a 40-foot pond was excavated, and gravel was added next to the house. Jane also brought lots of plants from her previous home and has planted hundreds of bulbs over the last two years, with Blin overseeing her work.

The surrounding farmland is arable land with sheep and beef cattle, and there is lots of wildlife, including owls, woodpeckers, nuthatches, and pheasants, as well as wild deer roaming freely. There are two beautiful old churches nearby, one of them being St George's which is the farmers' church that holds harvest festivals and thanksgiving services, making the Black Barn a very enchanting place to live for Jane and Blin.

ABOVE *Another of Blin's preferred spots, Jane's bed, is in a sun-filled room with quaint echoes of the fact it was originally a barn, making it a special and unique environment. A cowhide Arne Jacobsen chair sits in the corner, a touch of new style mixed with the old.*

OPPOSITE *This wonderful treehouse was built around the old oak tree to the north of the property. Blin is so lucky to live here and enjoy the space and all that the garden and surrounding woodland have to offer.*

"Bonnie is saint-like, hates to do anything wrong, and food is her life. Bessie is not saint-like, loves to do anything wrong, and ignores instructions."

BONNIE AND BESS— COTTAGE CHIC

OPPOSITE *On the soft Berber rug, a comfy ottoman offers a place for Bess to relax. A pop of color is provided by the yellow armchair. Hanging above it is one of Milly's pieces of art.*

PAGE 72 *Both dogs make use of the rugs—Bess on the sheepskin rug on a hide ottoman, Bonnie on the hide rug on the floor. The stunning abstract painting above them complements the warm interior colors and original floorboards.*

PAGE 73 TOP *A leather club chair sits in the bay window, with wooden slatted blinds pulled up to allow the sun to flood in, making this a relaxing place to sit.*

PAGE 73 BOTTOM *The very striking green-painted wall brings everything together. Again we see the yellow adding a pop of color to the earth tones of Jill's chosen palette. A large fiddle-leaf fig plant with its glossy leaves adds texture to this space.*

Bonnie and Bess live in Richmond in southwest London, surrounded by meadows and parkland, with Jill and her daughter Milly. Residing in a beautiful cottage with a large garden, these two Labrador Retrievers live a pretty wonderful life.

Bonnie was born in Chiswick, west London, and is nine years old, while Bess is from north London and is three years old. Bess's sole purpose is to annoy Bonnie, but Bonnie is a very good-natured dog and doesn't get cross. They make a very striking pair of dogs in their contrasting blond and black coats.

Their daily routine involves a long walk out onto the woodland or up to Richmond Park nearby, which has many dog-walking opportunities with 2,500 acres of stunning space. Both dogs love to sleep and, as Labrador Retrievers, they live to eat. Labradors are the most popular dog in the UK, US, and Canada, thanks to their lovely nature. However, with their high energy, it's necessary to train them, otherwise they get out of control. Bessie has

proved difficult to train; she is definitely of the opinion that if there's nothing in it for her, then she will ignore instructions.

Jill has lived in the house for 18 years. Originally a 17th-century cottage, it is built on a site that was once a flax field. Renovations are ongoing, and I really like what Jill has achieved; it is bright and contemporary, yet comfort is key. The color palette of green and soft brown with highlights of yellow makes it bang up to date, breathing real life into this old cottage.

With an open-plan layout, all the rooms flow from one to the other. The two living rooms open out onto the kitchen and conversatory, and are all about relaxing; comfortable sofas and soft rugs make the space easy. Bonnie and Bess are allowed in most places in the house, and although they

have their own beds, they can usually be found on the sofas or in the bedrooms.

The kitchen is functional but fashionable; the black fixtures, open shelves, and green marble splash back are striking. Jill mostly entertains in the conservatory: an all-year-round indoor garden, filled with plants, which is magical for supper parties. In the evenings, candles can be lit to illuminate the outdoor garden, adding even more to the atmosphere.

Milly is an artist, and various examples of her work are seen throughout the house, mixed with other pieces of art. Upstairs there are three bedrooms, and Jill's bedroom, with en suite bathroom, looks out onto the garden.

One feels embedded in the country here, but it's actually very easy to reach London and the nearby town of Kingston.

Sadly, since we took these pictures, Bonnie died after a short illness. I asked Jill for some words about her: "She was the most beautiful, loving, and loyal dog we have ever known."

PAGES 74–75 *In the open-plan kitchen, the sky light adds even more brightness. Bess sits on this small green sofa, which, along with the green marble splash back, brings in the palette of the rest of the house.*

OPPOSITE *The conservatory is at the back of the house and brings the outside in with lots of plants and a flagstone floor. It is a very warm, cocoon-like space for entertaining.*

ABOVE *Jill's bedroom is also at the rear of the house—the French doors open onto the garden below. Bonnie and Bess are very at home on the bed. Above the bed is a piece of hand-cut sculpture by Milly.*

RIGHT *Bonnie can be seen running through the beautiful garden; Jill is a keen gardener, and what once was a flax field is now an enviably lush space.*

SMITH, RONNIE, RITA, RUBY, AND LENNY— BOHEMIAN STYLE

These five extraordinary dogs, all of whom have had a remarkable start in life, live with Nikki Tibbles in her two homes. For this photography shoot we were at her country residence in the small town of Petworth in West Sussex. The house is stunning and the back section was built in 1700, with the front added in 1800.

As well as being a luxury florist, Nikki has founded a rescue dog organization, and I will talk more about the charity in the Rescue Dogs chapter (see pages 156-173). Nikki's story inspired me to include the charity chapter and do what I can in any small way to bring to the attention of my readers the plight of so many dogs around the world.

I loved the time I spent with these five dogs—their characters shone through very quickly and it helped us decide who would be good for each picture, as we

OPPOSITE *The living room sits at the front of the house, and features the original old floorboards with bold, colorful rugs. Everywhere you look there are interesting objects, and this room has a strong color theme. Ronnie is lying on the particularly striking sofa.*

came to know who would sit still and who would do what they were told. Sometimes one or two of them followed us around, just to be nosey.

Smith, who has a very distinctive red coat and sharp pointed ears, is named after the man who found him. A DNA test has shown he is a mix of Belgian Shepherd and Finnish Spitz. Nikki describes him as a gorgeous, gentle soul. He is 12½ years old now. He came from Spain where he was found half-dead in a puddle. After having been kept in a cage for three years, he had a shattered collarbone, eardrum, and ribs. He was driven across to the UK and, after having rotten teeth removed, he began his slow progression to health and happiness.

Ronnie is a gentle giant from Romania. He was one of a litter of puppies and his DNA shows he is probably a mix of Caucasian Shepherd and Magyar Agár (a type of sighthound). His mother was found dead, having been shot, and Ronnie is slightly hard of hearing, probably due to having been near gunshots. He is five years old.

Rita is two and a half years old and likely a crossbreed from Puerto Rico. As with all the dogs, she fits into the family and is a

LEFT *Ruby and Rita sit in front of the fire, around which the original wooden mantelpiece and exposed brick provide a focal point. The paneled walls have been painted pale blue and many other shades of blue are reflected throughout the rest of the room.*

loving pet. Nikki first encountered her in Puerto Rico where her charity had set up a dog sterilization program for low-income families. Rita literally fitted into Nikki's hand—she had the waggiest tail with the most extraordinary looks. Nikki took Rita back to her hotel, and then to Los Angeles for health checks before bringing her to the UK.

Ruby is also around two and a half years old and from Puerto Rico, and is most likely a Ridgeback. Her story is similar to Rita's—after Nikki found her,

she was taken to Los Angeles for health checks and then brought to the UK. She is a gentle, loving soul.

Lenny is almost 11 years old and was found in a dry well in Spain when he was only six months old, along with a Rottweiler. He is from a livestock guarding breed, indicated by the extremely thick skin around his neck. He has big, doleful eyes and an adorable character.

When the dogs are all together in Petworth, they have the run of around

OPPOSITE & ABOVE *This cozy nook for reading and relaxing is at the back of the house. A large vintage bookcase with books arranged by color makes for an impressive display. Ruby sits on a green midcentury chair as Smith enters the room. I love the scale of the large paintings beneath the window.*

15 acres of land. They are taken for long walks by Nikki, or Alcina who works with her, or they are allowed simply to roam around the house.

Petworth is a small town, nestled in the heart of the South Downs National Park and about an hour from London. The town has a rich history and a reputation for being a leading antique center. It is only a short drive away from the beautiful south coast.

As a florist of international status, Nikki surrounds herself with striking colors. She creates the most unique and outstanding installations for her customers and clients, so it's no surprise that this creative

LEFT *Upstairs in the main bedroom Ruby lies on the ottoman opposite the bed. A clever mix of pillows beneath the vintage paintings ties the color scheme together. Sisal and wool rugs over the floorboards add warmth, and light floods through the big windows.*

OPPOSITE *Lenny is sleeping on the soft rug in the master bedroom. More vintage floral pictures hang beside the small fireplace. Nikki has a thoughtful way of mixing colors, styles, and items from different periods together.*

passion for vibrant tones and a bold esthetic is reflected in every room in the house. She has a love of vintage items, but this is also sharply contrasted by modern art and rugs.

Nikki loves to live in a beautiful environment and having her dogs share her life doesn't stop her—they go pretty much where they like and follow her everywhere. They have been known to all get on her bed at once.

RIGHT *Three stunning Missoni rugs cover the painted floor in this spare room. Pale pink walls and exposed beams add heaps of character. The glorious yellow upholstered chair and vibrant pillows are a masterful touch.*

LEFT *Rita and Ruby wait patiently outside the back door to be let back in the house. A champagne bowl is used as a drinking vessel for the dogs.*

OPPOSITE *Unaware of all the fuss while we arrange pillows and straighten the throw, Smith dozes on the cream-painted Provençal Louis XV bed. I love how the dogs are all so relaxed and completely at home.*

> " Coco is loyal and loving, but slightly eccentric at times. "

COCO—MODERN NEUTRAL HOME

OPPOSITE *Coco sits on the sofa in the wide, open space that is for dining, cooking, and relaxing. On the vintage elm console table against the window are two tall iron figurines, with three bowls adding to the rustic display. The painting on the wall to the right is by Susan Caines.*

Coco is a Cocker Spaniel with a blue roan coat. Her name was inspired by Coco Chanel, after the iconic fashion designer's little black suits and pearl necklaces. She is four years old and lives with Bryony and Nigel in their home in Oxshott, Surrey. Surrey, in the southeast of England, is a very popular area as it has a higher proportion of woodland than any other county, four racecourses, and the famous golf course of Wentworth. A short train ride into London makes the location perfect for commuters.

Coco started her life in Yorkshire, where she had a huge amount of land attached to the house to roam as well as the rolling hills nearby. A year ago, Bryony and Nigel moved south to this beautiful part of Surrey; instead of the green hills, she now has wooded areas surrounding the house, and is taken most days for long walks into the woodland.

She is allowed around the whole house and likes being with humans—she often jumps up onto the bed in the morning. Although described as eccentric, like all dogs,

she is incredibly loyal and motivated by food. With a sleek coat and big soulful eyes, Coco lives up to her namesake. She is playful and enjoys running around in the garden.

The house is 10 years old and although they have lived there for a year, the couple are still in the throes of decorating, experimenting with color on the walls, learning how to use each room, and choosing the perfect furnishings. The house is very light and modern and flows well from room to room. Bryony and Nigel's style is neutral and clean, with a touch of vintage that adds character. Moving from

an old house in Yorkshire to this house has meant a shift of style and figuring out what will work. Most of the furniture was left in Yorkshire, so at the moment their home is a work in progress, but from day one it has felt right; the move to be nearer to family has been seamless and they haven't looked back.

The main living space on the ground floor has a huge kitchen with a central island unit that had been left by the previous owners. This has been repainted and includes new doors and furniture to update it, so it fits more with their style. From there are doors to the garden and to the left a comfortable area for watching television or relaxing with a book. Bryony and Nigel entertain frequently and have bought a huge rectangular dining table and chairs, endorsing the fact that this space is the heartbeat of the house; the very high ceilings with lots of windows make it cheerful, even on the dullest of days. This room is the one they spend most time in, but during the summer months they eat outside every night.

Spanning three floors with five bedrooms, the house offers plenty of room for guests to stay without feeling claustrophobic. Bryony has also created a dressing room on the first floor close to the master bedroom, a functional space with plenty of light and, most importantly, mirrors.

Bryony and Nigel love living here, and having Coco in their lives makes it pretty perfect.

The afternoon sun filters through the shutters onto the bed in the spare room, making this one of Coco's favorite spots for snoozing.

OPPOSITE *The large garden is enough for Coco when she is not being taken out to the nearby woodland. The covered dining area is used a lot during summer evenings and is sheltered from the wind and rain.*

SHORESIDE DOGS

PERCY, JOE AND JARVIS, SID AND PIP, ALBERT AND RAF, GEORGE

> " Percy is such an easy-going dog with only one foible—he won't lie on hard floors. Percy loves everyone."

PERCY— HERITAGE HOME

OPPOSITE *Percy lies languidly on the rug, sun streaming through the window, in the skilfully designed new kitchen installed by the owners, with bespoke worktops and a deep butler's sink with brass taps.*

PAGE 98 TOP *The main living space is found upstairs, and is a huge bright room looking out onto the old High Street. The two dark green velvet sofas provide a chill out space for the family. Striking, beautifully pleated yellow velvet curtains illustrate the owners' unique use of color.*

Percy is a rather elegant young Whippet, 13 months old at the time these photographs were taken. When his owners were ready to get a dog, they contacted the owner of a black Whippet they had met a few years earlier; fortunately her dog had sired a litter that had been born just days earlier. This is the first time they have owned a dog, but it was love at first sight and they have never looked back.

Percy's home is in Hastings, a town on England's south-east coast, famously known for the Battle of Hastings fought in 1066 on a nearby field, where Battle Abbey stands. The Norman ruins of Hastings Castle overlook the waters of the English Channel.

Percy doesn't like early mornings and takes a while to get going. He goes for a short walk after breakfast and then follows his owners around the house, with short bursts of rough and tumble with toys. At lunchtime he has a longer walk, on the east hill or on the beach at low tide. As Hastings is so dog-friendly, he has many canine chums, including Bonnie the Greyhound and Pablo the Italian

Greyhound. They meet up and play frequently and he is well known in town. His favorite pub is the First In Last Out, because they have an open fire. Around 6pm Percy eats dinner and afterward lies on the couch, spending the evening relaxing with his owners.

Percy's owners, a fashion buyer and a property restoration specialist, found this spectacular Regency/late Georgian house in the old town of Hastings, which has one of the most diverse ranges of housing stock in the country; Georgian town houses sit alongside medieval timbered houses and fisherman's cottages, and no two houses are

LEFT *In the dining room, Percy's bed is strategically placed against the radiator. He likes to be wherever his owners are. Painted floorboards, warm colored walls, and retro dining chairs with bright seat covers create an eclectic space.*

Percy relaxing on the couch in the living space, where everyone gets together at the end of the day. A warm mix of textiles, a vintage coffee table, and gilt-framed art make a unique statement.

OPPOSITE *Percy's favorite spot in the home office—as long as there is company. This space functions well for working from home: the Vitsœ shelving system, designed by Dieter Rams in 1960 and still manufactured today, provides order and there's an authentic Eames office chair, bought on eBay.*

BELOW & RIGHT *The master bedroom is on the top floor of the house. Percy will come up here to stand on the couch and do his "nosy neighbor" impersonation, watching the activity on the busy street below.*

the same. Their house was listed as a gentleman's residence, and has four floors.

They bought the house five years ago, and it soon became apparent that the roof was leaking. All the plumbing and electrics had to be replaced, two new bathrooms and a new kitchen were installed, and the floorboards were sanded and painted, before the house was ready for some serious interior design. Now it has a very tasteful and comfortable feel, with a clever use of paint color and textiles, plus art and objects collected from a year spent living in Paris.

Percy lives harmoniously with his owners in the house and is allowed to roam freely throughout. Like so many of our dogs, he is the heart of this home.

> "Joe and Jarvis often go to watch Hastings United football team; they were official match sponsors this season."

JOE AND JARVIS— VIBRANT CONVERSION

OPPOSITE *This huge room, formerly the billiard room, has a large light well that floods the space with natural light. Joe and Jarvis bask in the warm glow of the lights from the neon sign, one of the many bespoke signs created by the owner.*

Joe and Jarvis, named after Joe Cocker and Jarvis Cocker, are both obviously Cocker Spaniels, born on Halloween nine years ago. They came from a breeder in Barnstaple, Devon in the southwest of England, and now live in St Leonards-on-Sea with their owners, Philip and Olivia. St Leonards is on the south coast of England. Each morning they have a stroll along the promenade, but are always on a leash, as otherwise they go straight into the sea and swim toward France. This did happen once, and thankfully the beach patrol and coastguard rescued Joe and Jarvis when they were a mile out to sea.

Although they are siblings, they have very different characters. Joe loves food and to play, and always carries a toy with him on a walk. Jarvis is less interested in food and more of a diva—he's the first to complain and always wants to be picked up and cuddled. Both dogs love meaty bones, chicken, rice, and minced beef, but never eat canned food. They are orange roan in color and are

You can just see the light well above the living room—this gives a sense of the height of the room. A neon hangman's noose adds humor. A vintage gurney provides a base for the dining table and the circus stands act as seats. These are the original herringbone floorboards.

extremely attractive dogs. Originally bred as gun dogs, they are good-natured and make perfect pets.

Philip and Olivia have lived at The Admiral Benbow for ten years, a converted pub. It started its life as the Saxon Shades public house in 1833, latterly became the Yorkshire Grey, and finally The Admiral Benbow in the 1990s. In 1800, it housed horses in its stables in the yard which regularly pulled carriages to Folkestone, another coastal town. In 1901, the stables were built over with a billiard room. The first game of billiards that took place there was played by world champion George Stephenson in 1901. The billiards room was also used as a druids' lodge, a meeting place for an English fraternal organization, and eventually in the 1980s became Blades, which is believed to have been the first gay club in Hastings and St Leonards. The pub was closed for good in

ABOVE LEFT *Joe and Jarvis sit rather elegantly in their bespoke doghouse. This is such a wonderful image—they seem unfazed by all going on around them and are sitting patiently, waiting for the picture to be taken.*

ABOVE RIGHT *This far side of the living room features a collection of vintage finds, including an illuminated exit sign and layers of rugs on the floor. The chair, like the sofas, was upholstered by Bruce Robbins using vintage tapestries found in thrift shops. The door opens out onto the hallway.*

2008, after which it was purchased and became the extraordinary live/work space it is today.

Without doubt, from the outside it still looks as if it was originally a pub, but now it is painted in a dark color and the windows are obscured, which disguise the fact it is a home. When first walking into the space you cannot imagine what lies ahead—it is both unique and overwhelming. You might expect that it will be dark, but on the contrary it is both light and colorful. On folding the shutters back in the corner room there is an epic view of the sea and the light floods in, making it a space for Joe and Jarvis to chill while soaking up the sun.

Philip makes neon bespoke signs, hence the collections we see in the pictures, which sit alongside vintage circus items and many other

OPPOSITE *More characterful style with original old cinema seats and a vintage children's horse ride. The authentic neon signs add a glow to the space. The red painted door leads through to the long hallway.*

ABOVE *The quirky little staircase which leads up to the office. Note how the door has a curved bottom in line with the opening. The handrail is made from a vintage metal measuring tape.*

LEFT *This is the upstairs corner room, which looks directly out to the sea. The wallpaper is by Deborah Bowness and the two-seater sofa is Danish midcentury. A vintage amusements sign leans against the wall in the corner of the room.*

unusual items. He and Olivia have an eye for the extraordinary, making this home one in a million; at every corner you turn there is something intriguing. Among other things, they have built Joe and Jarvis their very own two-tier dog hut.

In the main living space there is a huge light well, along with comfortable sofas and chairs, making it ideal for relaxing, dining, and sitting. Velvet-covered old cinema seats, bright colors, and interesting art made this such an interesting and inspiring home to photograph.

Joe and Jarvis have landed on their feet.

ABOVE *The long upstairs hallway, with its original herringbone parquet floor, is illuminated by swirls of neon. Doors to the left lead off to the bathroom and kitchen, and the large living space is off to the right.*

LEFT *A walk along the seafront promenade is a daily ritual. Joe likes to take his favorite toy rabbit with him on walks, and has been known to carry it for miles at a time.*

OPPOSITE *In the spare bedroom, an old advertising poster for Hastings and St Leonards and an impressive trio of illuminated flying ducks are typical of the delightful surprises to be found in this house. Joe and Jarvis sit on the vintage bed, next to the shuttered window which overlooks the street below.*

> "Sid and Pip both sleep on our super-king-size bed every night, where there is room for all of us."

SID AND PIP—TOWN HOUSE APARTMENT

Sid and Pip live with Wayne and Adam in St Leonards-on-Sea, which is in the borough of Hastings in East Sussex. Sid is a Pug and is ten years old. Born in Essex, his show name is Prince Ebony and his father was from the Pugaran family, a Kennel Club assured breeder. His hobbies are sitting in the kitchen waiting for dinner, and eating small stones on the beach. Pip is five years old, born in High Wycombe in Buckinghamshire on Christmas Eve, and is a crossbreed of French Bulldog, Staffordshire Bull Terrier, and Pug. She likes to hunt squirrels by day and bark at any dog or animal on the television in the evening.

The dogs love living by the sea and are often taken to the beach for walks, or there is a lovely park opposite their apartment where they meet all their local canine chums for a play.

Wayne and Adam moved to St Leonards from London two years ago. Wayne owns and runs a pub, while Adam is a fashion lecturer. Their apartment is a conversion in a large Victorian town house by the architect James Burton.

OPPOSITE *The main living space in the apartment. The original fire surround has been painted white, as have the floorboards. The Louis XV mirror was found at furniture supplier The French Depot, and the art is by Harland Miller and Julie Verhoeven.*

PAGE 112 *This is Sid's normal sleeping position—chin down, paws out—while Pip poses with great elegance. The chest of drawers displays art by Sue Tilley and owls from the thrift store.*

PAGE 113 *Pip and Sid sit comfortably on the church pew inside the pub owned and run by Wayne. It is tastefully decorated with shelves filled with vintage finds.*

It is spacious with a garden and enormous bay windows looking out onto the park opposite. They have furnished it mainly with flea market and vintage finds from local stores, and they have displayed an eclectic mix of art by great friends of theirs.

Pip and Sid often go with Wayne to his pub, The Fountain; they attract lots of attention and fit right in with the decor.

"Albert and Raf are firm friends and play all day, from the moment they wake until sundown."

ALBERT AND RAF— MODERN BUNGALOW

OPPOSITE *Albert and Raf pose obediently with the vintage midcentury chairs. The light that comes in from the skylight above gives the dining space a great amount of energy. The sliding doors lead out to the sloping garden and up onto the Downs.*

PAGE 116 *The door opens out to the front garden. The dogs are rushing in for dinner after a hectic day tearing round the garden. The pristine white kitchen with black highlights also has a skylight.*

Albert and Raf are Cavapoos, also known as Cavadoodles—a cross between a female Cavalier King Charles Spaniel and a male Poodle. The breed is super friendly and the big bonus is that they are hypoallergenic and shed no hair whatsoever, which is great for black carpets. They live together with Richard and Graham in West Sussex on the south coast of England, just on the edge of the South Downs.

Albert is eight years old and was born in September 2011. Richard and Graham, who used to work in the fashion industry, named him after Alber Elbaz, the designer at fashion house Lanvin for a number of years. They got Albert when living in an apartment in Hove, also on the south coast, so he was brought up with daily trips to the sea and promenade at the end of the road. From an early age Albert loved the sea, mainly to cool off after a very hectic game of ball on the seashore. Six and a half years ago they moved to their current home, where they enjoy sea views and still have easy access to the coast by car.

Raf joined them as a puppy two years ago. Although he is also a Cavapoo, the mix in him seems more Spaniel than Poodle. He was born in south Wales in August 2017. Graham and Richard saw his puppy picture online while away on vacation, and on arriving home they drove five hours each way to collect him. He is also named after a favorite fashion designer of theirs, Raf Simons. Raf especially loves the water and took to swimming like a duck to water.

Albert and Raf bonded very well and are firm friends—having a canine companion has really energized Albert. Getting Raf was an excellent decision—bringing him all the way from Carmarthen was worth it.

LEFT *One of Richard's paintings, entitled "Tangle," hangs over the console. Pots and artefacts sit side by side, having been collected over the years and fitting in with the white and earth tones palette. The cream vase holds some dried grass picked up on the beach.*

ABOVE *Albert steps down from the black carpeted staircase. Another piece of Richard's art hangs on the black painted wall, creating a striking first impression when entering the house.*

RIGHT *Raf relaxes, elegantly contrasting the cream Egg chair by Arne Jacobsen. The sun streams through French doors, adding yet more light to this room.*

OPPOSITE *Above the sofa is "Message," another painting by Richard. The pillow is made from turn-of-the-19th-century German grain sacks. The tall African sculpture is part of their collection that they've moved from home to home; they've owned it for 25 years.*

Richard and Graham, who used to work in the fashion industry, live in this bright mid-20th century bungalow, which they have completely refurbished and modernized over the past few years, creating more space and adding sky lights. The white and neutral palette also fills the house with natural light.

The garden has been completely redesigned all around the house to create various seating and dining areas with distant views of the sparkling sea.

Albert and Raf are completely safe within the garden and use it as a constant play and excavating area. When it's dark and Richard and Graham look down at the twinkling lights in the village below; it reminds them of Los Angeles, inspiring them to nickname the house "Chaletfornia." With the natural beauty of the South Downs outside the back door, and the vibrancy of Brighton close by, they feel they have the best of both worlds.

As Richard now spends a lot of time painting, he has a studio with windows facing the sea, which provides the perfect bright, tranquil environment for his work. The house is filled with his art and is constantly evolving as his inspiration and paintings change and as they are sold.

Many of the artefacts in the house have been with them over the years as they have moved from location to location; they are items that have meaning for them and provide the core of their taste and style.

Bringing the dogs into their lives has been the best thing they've done; Albert and Raf have provided companionship, laughter, and joy.

ABOVE *Staying true to the neutral palette, this is another iconic design piece, the lounge chair by Charles and Ray Eames. The chair and ottoman are made from plywood and leather.*

RIGHT *Albert and Raf run across the Downs with a ball; they love to play in the freedom of this magical space.*

OPPOSITE *Albert sits on the vintage Bergère chair under the painting by Richard, "Mask with Bird." Raf relaxes on the bed with a "hippy" bedspread they've had since the 1970s.*

> "George is the legend of the lagoon that's behind the house; people love to watch him swim for hours."

GEORGE—HOUSE BY THE MARINA

George is a German Wirehaired Pointer, bred to hunt, point, and retrieve. He is 11 years old and lives with Judy and Peter in Poole in Dorset. A large town on the south coast of England, Poole is popular for wind and kite surfing. George's Kennel Club name is Muntjac Jack and his mother was born and bred from a line of hunting dogs in the New Forest and Wareham Forest. He uses his hunting abilities to watch the sea bass feeding and jumping in the lagoon behind the house.

He loves people and greets them when on his daily walks in the New Forest—he is definitely a local celebrity around the area. Judy says he has been the best companion and the most wonderful dog.

Judy, who works in retail, and Peter, an architect, have lived in Salterns Marina for many years. The marina is one of the most expensive and is the closest to the mouth of Poole Harbour, which is one of the biggest natural harbors in the world. Salterns was a former landing stage for passengers from BOAC (British Overseas Airways

OPPOSITE *The kitchen, positioned at the front of the house, steps down directly onto the marina. It has recently been remodeled with stainless steel cupboards and gilt handles. George can be seen just finishing his lunch.*

Each balcony, like the one George is sitting on, looks straight out onto the lagoon, making this one of the most desirable views in Poole. The houses are purposely designed to fit in with their surroundings.

Corporation) sea planes—they would be taken from there to the Harbour Heights hotel. The sea planes were moored in the lagoon.

The group of houses that Peter and Judy live in was formerly part of the marina and built some 20 years ago. Their house has stunning views across the harbor to Brownsea Island, a beautiful area with a wealth of wildlife, and boasts breathtaking sunsets. The water can be accessed directly via a private dock on the lagoon. The house has four floors and four bedrooms, two of which have balconies with amazing views of the lagoon.

George is taken to the local beaches, including Branksome Dene, which is a beach that dogs are unusually allowed on all year round. He loves to swim and runs into the water all the time. He is extremely well trained and obeys the whistle signal, making it easy to take photographs of him, but like all dogs he is also motivated by food. He is a handsome, well-behaved dog that lives a truly active life in this environment.

A large printed cowhide rug covers the cool tiles on the living room floor. George is taking a rest after hours of swimming in the lagoon. The double doors open out onto the patio, which has steps down to the lagoon.

BELOW *The row of houses with striking rooftops look out over the lagoon and beyond onto the open sea.*

OPPOSITE TOP LEFT AND RIGHT
George runs along the beach at Branksome Dene. It is extremely popular with dog owners as dogs are permitted all year round. The deck is George's favorite spot for surveying the lagoon, on the lookout for signs of life.

OPPOSITE BOTTOM LEFT AND RIGHT *The dock with a small boat gives direct access to the water, which is George's favorite place. George's love of water is common knowledge amongst the residents of the houses surrounding the marina.*

DESIGN DOGS

KIBA, FLO AND IVY, MILO, OTIS, AND HARDY

"Kiba is a social butterfly; she always treats visitors with an enthusiastic welcome. She has a special rapport with the mailman."

KIBA—HISTORIC MANOR HOUSE

OPPOSITE *In this impressive entrance hall, Kiba makes her way down the grand staircase, delighted at having been allowed upstairs. A rather elegant female bust on a plinth looks perfectly in place against the leaded windows.*

Kiba is seven years old, and is one of four sisters born locally. She is a Japanese Spitz, which is a small dog, but is said to have the heart of a guard dog, and is larger than its small cousin the Pomeranian. She lives with Tania, Duncan, and their grown-up children in their house in East Sussex, which lies in the center of an Area of Outstanding Natural Beauty (a designated exceptional landscape) and is only a short distance from the coastal towns of St Leonards-on-Sea and Hastings.

Kiba's full name is Shiroi Kiba, which means "white fang" in Japanese—she was named after a character in the anime series Naruto by Tania and Duncan's son when he was small. She is not a typical country dog, but she does a very good impersonation of one. She chases rabbits, barks ferociously at the birds and bees, and loves to run through the fields, although she keeps her immaculate white coat clean largely by herself.

Daily life at home is always busy and Kiba likes to be involved. She is an outstanding guard dog and is protective

of her home, although she has her special rapport with the mailman and also greets regular visitors with a warm welcome, especially if rewarded with a treat. When it comes to downtime, she loves the cool stone floor of the courtyard and on winter evenings a snooze by the fire, but always seeks the company of the family. At night she loves to spend time with the family's Burmese cat—even if the friendship is not always reciprocated, Kiba is never far from her side.

The house and grounds are stunning and extremely impressive on arrival, with a long, sweeping drive and a magnificent view of the rolling hills from the front of the house. The house itself is one of the most historic in southeast England, dating back to the 13th century. Underneath its Georgian exterior lies a timber-framed Tudor manor house that has been home to many families over the years. Some interesting characters have owned the house, including the family that inspired Shakespeare's King Lear and a baron who saved the life of a young Queen Victoria. The house is a Grade 2 listed building,

OPPOSITE *This warm spot by the open fire is a hit with Kiba. The sweeping staircase provides a "wow" factor when entering the house, especially combined with the paneled walls and the stunning fireplace.*

ABOVE *The long dining table and Louis Ghost chairs by Philippe Starck for Kartell give a certain modern feeling but hold on to the traditional look. The magnificent Baccarat crystal chandelier adds opulence to the space.*

meaning it is of special architectural interest and as such there are restrictions on any amendments. With nine bedrooms and several outbuildings, it's a large home. On our photography shoot day Kiba was allowed to go through the whole house and pose in each of its rooms; she seemed to rather enjoy it, and I'm sure it's because she is never normally allowed upstairs.

Tania and Duncan have a keen eye for interiors and, although simple in design and taste, the effect is very impressive. The dining table can seat over 20 people, but equally works well for a few. The round table in the entrance hall extends and makes an alternative dining space. It is extremely cozy at Christmas time with the fire burning. The large living space with floor-to-ceiling windows and comfortable sofas is an

LEFT *Kiba makes herself at home on the leather sofa. This smaller room that leads off the kitchen is a more intimate environment, perfect for watching television or reading.*

The main living room, with two large sofas and armchairs, features vast doors that open out onto the garden, which make this room truly appealing in the summer. Being able to move from house to garden is ideal for entertaining.

excellent space for hosting guests, while the smaller room that leads off the kitchen is ideal for suppers in front of the television. The layout and size of both the house and garden make them perfect for parties and entertaining. When you have a home as unique as this, it's good to share it with others.

While making the house their own is an ongoing project and seems almost impossible to complete, Tania and Duncan love it and it almost feels impossible for them to leave. It is their home, and there are plenty of things to enjoy and discover while this vast project continues.

OPPOSITE *One of the spare bedrooms at the back of the house. Sitting on the polished and stained floorboards is a freestanding Catchpole and Rye bath. Kiba sits on a vintage leather trunk at the base of the bed.*

ABOVE LEFT *A second refurbished spare bedroom, with simple styling but impressive furniture. A copper Catchpole and Rye bath adds warmth to the room.*

ABOVE RIGHT *This semi-derelict outbuilding, with no roof and weathered walls, is earmarked for renovation as part of the ongoing work on this stunning property and its grounds.*

RIGHT *The contrast of Kiba in the middle of the fallen leaves from this acer tree is so striking that she could almost be in Japan. Looking at the garden from the kitchen, this tree looks like flames.*

> "Although they are sisters, they have quite different characters; Flo is bright, stubborn, and moody, while Ivy is very pretty and not as clever as Flo, but loves everyone."

FLO AND IVY— RENOVATED SCHOOLHOUSE

Flo and Ivy are Maltipoos, a cross between Maltese Terriers and Poodles, and came from a breeder in Colchester, Essex. They have the same parents but were born seven months apart: Flo was born in November 2010 and Ivy was born in June 2011. Ivy is very sociable and will be quick to give you a lick, whilst Flo tends to be slightly more discerning.

They live with Marilyn and Julyan in Bourne End, Buckinghamshire, a village flanked by countryside and woodland. During the day the dogs are taken for several walks: one big walk into the woods, then shorter walks on the village green. They live a comfortable life and share the attention of Marilyn and Julyan.

Marilyn's business is in design, and the house is decorated no differently from how it would be without dogs, aside from a throw here or there. Ivy and Flo have access to all areas and get to sit on some pretty remarkable furniture. They also have the garden with

OPPOSITE *Flo and Ivy are sitting on the dining bench, ready to join in with whatever meal is happening. Huge windows bring the garden into the space and fill it with natural light. The long metal dining table seats the largest of dinner parties.*

a stream running through it, so there is plenty of wildlife for them to watch and chase.

Flo and Ivy live a dual life as they spend much time in France in Marilyn and Julyan's second home. Julyan drives them there over a two-day period; the dogs completely know the drill and even preempt what direction to take when arriving at the overnight hotel.

Their French home is in the village of Valros in the commune of Hérault in southern France. While there, they enjoy trips to the beach—they love to play with a ball on the beach, but when it gets too hot, they dig a hole in the sand under the lounger. The village itself has a beautiful old church that sits opposite their house in the square and the bells ring out every hour very loudly, but the dogs don't even flinch. I'm convinced the dogs are bilingual!

Marilyn and Julyan moved into their English house in 1997. It was an old schoolhouse which has had extensive renovation and has taken on many guises over the years. Now it is bright, open, and minimalist; natural fabrics, stone, metal, and concrete are the

OPPOSITE *A garden room extension on the back of the house with metal windows and doors. Flo and Ivy's feeding area is on the stone floor.*

ABOVE *The bespoke linen sofa was made by Bray Design, and the green painting is by Richard Nott. An Italian olive pot is used as a vase on the vintage raw elm coffee table.*

ABOVE *Flo walks down the stairs, past a selection of original African masks bought from the market in Sablon, Belgium.*

In this big open space, two bespoke linen L-shaped sofas have been made to fit the shape of the room. The raw elm coffee tables have been pushed together, and a hide-covered chair complements the natural décor. The two swirl paintings are by Richard Nott.

materials of choice that make it the cool and stylish interior that it is today. In her day-to-day life, Marilyn helps her clients to make design and fabric choices, so she's constantly exposed to the newest, most current trends when she travels to interior design fairs and fabric showrooms for research.

Upstairs, there are two bedrooms, both with bathrooms, and a loft space for closets. The dogs spend nighttime asleep on

OPPOSITE *Flo lies on the bed—this is definitely one of her favorite places. Large windows have been added to allow in the maximum amount of light. The dress picture above the bed is again by Richard Nott.*

the beds; although small, they make very good guard dogs and alert their owners if there are any noises.

Flo and Ivy are the first dogs Marilyn and Julyan have had and they now can't imagine life without them; they get on well together and are a big part of family life.

LEFT *Ivy loves to sleep on the bed. This room features shades of burnt orange and blue, while the walls are in a natural hue. The cupboards are covered in gray linen and have metal handles.*

ABOVE *Behind Ivy and Flo, who are catching some sunshine in the garden, is a small stream that attracts lots of wildlife. The dogs have become accustomed to this kind of activity.*

> " Every day the dogs have a mad half-hour belting around the garden, drinking from the pond and often jumping in, before collapsing onto their sofa. "

MILO, OTIS, AND HARDY— RIVER COTTAGES

Martin and Yvonne, along with their children Casper and Francesca, have lived in this house for 25 years. Milo, a Blue Belton Setter, joined them as a puppy nearly 12 years ago, from a breeder near Peterborough. Four years later a second puppy arrived—Otis is also a Blue Belton Setter, although with more black in his coat, from a breeder in Gloucestershire. Eighteen months ago Hardy joined the gang, but his story is quite different. He was an unwanted working dog, and although he is also a setter he is referred to as an Orange Belton working setter. Read more about Hardy's story on page 166.

Each day all three dogs are taken for a long walk in the woods and parkland near the house. Most days Yvonne takes them, and at weekends Martin will walk them to relax. Claudia, who helps to look after the dogs, will take them to the coast for a swim or up into the hills of Surrey, when Yvonne and Martin are away. Claudia adores the dogs, as they do her. The dogs also have the use of the

OPPOSITE *Otis relaxes on a yellow linen sofa. This part of the house is very modern, with Italian side tables bought from furniture brand Baxter and simple ceramics.*

Milo and Otis's very distinguished profiles are reflected in the vintage mirrored credenza, artfully blending in with the monochrome palette. A vintage swan from Josephine Ryan Antiques echoes the colors of the painting hanging above it.

ABOVE *The dogs sit on their own newly-laundered blue linen couch in the big family kitchen. Exposed original beams and white walls make the room fresh and bright. The original oil painting behind them complements the room beautifully.*

RIGHT *Milo peeks out from behind the concrete partition wall in the modern side of the home. Milo struggles to climb the open wooden stairs these days. An abstract piece of art from Josephine Ryan Antiques hangs opposite the foot of the stairs.*

house's large, beautifully-planted garden, with a pond which they love to swim in and drink from.

The dogs mostly hang out in the big kitchen and have their own couch that fits all three of them. Hardy quite often retreats to the dog crate, a place in which he feels comfortable and protected.

Martin and Yvonne's home is in Richmond, a beautiful, green area of southwest London, adjoining the River Thames. The house is a Georgian cottage built in 1730. After living there for five years, they also bought the cottage next door and

PAGES 150–151 *This majestic room, where Hardy sits, is a beautiful blend of both modern and vintage. The contemporary Italian sofas (one upholstered in red vintage fabric) are from Baxter. The giant Venetian mirror from the Decorative Antiques Fair in London is complemented by the Italian white table and chair, also both from Baxter.*

ABOVE *In the other half of the big room, on the dark wall two Venetian mirrors hang in the alcoves either side of the fireplace. To the left, a stunning tryptic sits above a dark wood console table.*

then proceeded to merge the two into one home, including the garden, which then gained the benefit of a beautiful old brick wall to the side.

The very distinctive interior style merges vintage and modern beautifully. The owners' skill is evident in how the two cottages have been blended together so well but are unique in look and feel.

Yvonne likes to start with a white background and neutral furniture as a base before she does anything, allowing herself the opportunity to change the environment easily. Color goes into soft furnishings, flowers, paintings, and decorative pieces, and she opts for those found in nature: green, chartreuse, nude, pinky reds, and woad-dyed antique linen (woad is a plant dye) in shades of pale blue and indigo. Stunning art is evident all through the home—in fact, they are running out of walls to hang it on.

Above all else it is a family home and also very clearly a party house: Martin and Yvonne are well known for opening their home to friends in aid of

The chartreuse yellow wall in the piano room is vibrant and striking. This clever use of color complements the antique Collard and Collard piano. A modern B&B Italia chair and stool, also upholstered in yellow, are the perfect match.

charities close to their hearts. Attention to detail and unique themes make these occasions coveted calendar dates for their guests. The garden is also opened to visitors to raise money for charity.

Yvonne is a true visionary and works hard to achieve perfection—her attention to detail is evident in everything you see. The home is beautiful but very comfortable, in an easy, relaxing style, and the dogs are very much part of it.

BELOW *A green velvet throw on Francesca's bed contrasts sharply with the dark wall behind it. Bedside tables in raw wood with old slate tops were bought from Petersham Nurseries.*

OPPOSITE *The stunning garden, designed by Yvonne. The dogs enjoy the space and the pond. The garden statues are from Josephine Ryan Antiques. The modern courtyard is where the two original cottages meet, at the back of house.*

RESCUE DOGS

EDDIE, FLYNN, PEGGY, MONKEY, HARDY, RONNIE AND LENNY, RUBY AND RITA, SMITH

EDDIE

Eddie is our second rescue dog from Battersea Dogs and Cats Home, one of the most well-known animal rescue homes. Although I had never been a dog owner in my life, my daughter badgered me to get one from almost the age she could talk, although it did take until she was nine years old for me to give in! There was never really any question that it was going to be a rescue dog; living in southwest London so close to Battersea, it was the natural choice. All these years later, I've learned a lot and I wouldn't do it any other way.

For obvious reasons, vetting has to take place when you adopt a rescue dog, and it really does help you make the decision. You have to consider if you will be able to walk the dog every day, whether you can make sure he or she is only left alone for a minimum amount of time, if the dog will be okay around children, and so on; it's common sense, really.

Eddie lives with me, but is shared with my daughter and her family. Since we have had Eddie, two grandchildren have been born and he is both tolerant and protective. I love how the children respond to him and learn how to take care of him; we all go to the park together, play together, and sleep together.

FLYNN

Mark and Andrew rescued and rehomed Flynn from All Dogs Matter, a charity for rescuing and rehoming dogs in the London area, although they also find homes for dogs from various countries outside the UK. Their mission is to transform the lives of unwanted dogs, finding them happy and safe forever homes.

Flynn was rescued after being found abandoned in a flat with three other dogs. He is now an integral part of Mark and Andrew's household, having slotted right in; he has a large personality and, although small, has big ideas. It was a match made in heaven; a happy ending to what could have been a very sad outcome.

Part of taking a dog into your home is making provision for when you are at work or on vacation. When the family are not available, Flynn goes for his daily walk with Waggy Walkers, a local doggy daycare provider—Flynn adores them. There are many doggy daycare and walkers available nowadays, and it is always important to meet them in person and get references before making a choice.

If Mark and Andrew are away on vacation, a good friend of theirs, Ian, moves into the house to take care of Flynn. Ian and Flynn have a great bond and it is the perfect arrangement for everyone.

PEGGY

Peggy came from Lurcher SOS, a Surrey-based Lurcher and Greyhound rescue center. The center rehabilitates and rehomes abandoned and abused Lurchers, Greyhounds, and Whippets. All dogs are placed in safe, caring foster homes until a permanent home is found.

Peggy was lucky to be rehomed by Ella and her husband Magnus. She fell on her feet, or should I say rug, as she is now the personality of Ella's shop in east London, A New Tribe, which imports rugs from Morocco among other things. Peggy likes nothing more to languidly lie on them. She is the center of attention from the customers and gets lots of affection. Ella has even created a hashtag for photos of her: #peggyonarug.

She is walked regularly in all the parks east London has to offer, but likes nothing more than lying on Ella and Magnus's bed or getting her tummy rubbed. I think there is a mutual love affair between her and her owners.

MONKEY

Monkey is eight years old and believed to be a Miniature Schnauzer crossed with a Poodle, although that is unconfirmed, as the dog rescue center had no information about his father. He came from Many Tears Animal Rescue, which is based in Carmarthenshire, Wales. Unusually, they primarily take in and rehome ex-breeding dogs who are no longer required.

Many Tears Animal Rescue provides a safe and stable foster environment for the dogs to adapt to the outside world, which many of them have never seen before being rescued, while looking for suitable, permanent homes.

Monkey came to Abigail and Graham at nine months old. Having already been through five homes at such an early stage of his life, he had massive separation anxiety issues—Abigail was unable to walk from one side of the room to the other without him following. However, slowly he grew in confidence and, with the help of his companion Myrtle, he plays and runs around all day.

He is now a very laid-back dog—Abigail says he is super chilled out. How lucky he is: he gets to hang out in a beautiful, comfortable home with people who love him.

HARDY

Hardy is about seven years old and is an ex-working dog from France. Unfortunately, it is only too frequent that working dogs are discarded after they are of no use to their owner. They have generally not been socialized and so require patient and understanding owners.

Hardy's rescuer drove for eight hours from Bordeaux to Calais to hand him over to his new owners, along with the necessary papers for crossing over into the UK. Unsurprisingly, Hardy was stressed and anxious, and it took a lot of patience, compassion, and hard work to get him to integrate into the family. Happily, he is slowly relaxing into daily life. He eats with the other dogs, but still prefers to retreat into his cage if he is feeling nervous or upset. He sometimes hides underneath furniture or in corners, but more and more will join his brothers together on the sofa. Hardy really is a beautiful dog and deserves the life he now has.

RONNIE AND LENNY

The adorable Lenny and Ronnie are two of Nikki Tibbles' own dogs. I've already described their tough start in life and how they have overcome hurdles that at first seemed unimaginable (see pages 78-87). They are loving, loyal and resilient, as are all dogs, which is one of the reasons we love our canine friends so much.

Nikki Tibbles is the founder of the Wild at Heart foundation, which funds and supports a variety of global projects to help further its mission to reduce the world's 600 million stray dog population. The foundation aims to do this through rehoming, sterilization, education, and awareness. Their inspiring tag line is "Believe in Dog."

RUBY AND RITA

One of the important aspects of Wild at Heart's mission is going into areas that have suffered natural disasters. Once there they work to provide veterinary care and surgery to help get dogs out of immediate danger. Ruby and Rita are both from Puerto Rico, which was devastated by Hurricane Maria in 2017. Having met Ruby and Rita through her work with Wild at Heart, Nikki very quickly welcomed them into her own rescue family, and they now live happily with her in the UK.

At present Wild at Heart helps to fund projects in 17 locations around the world. The foundation goes to countries in most need who have a fast-increasing stray dog population. Sterilization remains the single most effective and compassionate method to control the number of stray dogs. One litter of puppies born on the streets can result in 67,000 more strays in just six years.

Since 2015, the foundation has spayed and neutered 23,979 dogs, which has prevented the birth of up to 252 million stray, unwanted dogs. It also supports education projects in local communities to help them get to the root of the problem.

SMITH

With his very distinguished red coat, Smith is originally from Spain, and is the fifth member of Nikki's own tribe of rescue dogs.

Wild at Heart partner with a wide number of shelters globally to find homes for dogs that have been abandoned and neglected. These small organizations need all the help they can get to feed, treat, and sterilize dogs that are passing through their care. The foundation supports vital veterinary work and shelter maintenance, as well as finding suitable adopters. It's important to keep making space for the never-ending flow of dogs needing help. Since 2015, Wild at Heart has seen 1,360 dogs happily adopted.

Sadly, since these pictures were taken, Smith has passed away. Nikki says: "He was my true love. From the moment I saw this crumpled soul living in a cage, he has never left my side. He was my shadow."

Smith was an integral part of Nikki's rescue family and will be greatly missed.

INDEX

Page numbers in *italic* refer to captions.

RESOURCES

There are many organizations helping to rehome dogs to the right owners. Here are website addresses for some of them:

UK

Wild at Heart Foundation
www.wildatheartfoundation.org

Battersea
www.battersea.org.uk

Lurcher SOS Sighthound and Lurcher Rescue
www.lurchersos.org.uk

All Dogs Matter
alldogsmatter.co.uk

Many Tears Animal Rescue
www.manytearsrescue.org

Dogs Trust
www.dogstrust.org.uk

Royal Society for the Prevention of Cruelty to Animals (RSPCA)
www.rspca.org.uk

Blue Cross for Pets
www.bluecross.org.u

USA

Petfinder
www.petfinder.com

American Society for the Prevention of Cruelty to Animals (ASPCA)
www.aspca.org

Animal Lighthouse Rescue
www.alrcares.com

Animal Haven
animalhaven.org

Rescue Dogs Rock NYC
rescuedogsrocknyc.org

North Fork Animal Welfare League
main.nfawl.org

New York Bully Crew
nybullycrew.org

The Inner Pup
www.theinnerpup.org

CREDITS

CICO Books would like to thank the following dog owners for allowing us to photograph their homes:

Abigail Ahern (Monkey and Myrtle), *pages 40–48, 164–65*

Jill Baker (Bonnie and Bess), *pages 70–77*

Patrick Bushnell and Sheila Brown (Winnie and Flora), *pages 48–51*

Judy Cimdins (George), *pages 122–27*. Interior designed by Peter Donnelly.

Marilyn and Julyan Day (Flo and Ivy), *pages 138–45*

Deb and Rick Haylor (Alfie), *pages 56–61*

Jane Gates, garden designer (Blin), *pages 62–69*

Penny Horne (Bailey), *pages 52–53*

Bryony and Nigel Howes (Coco), *pages 88–93*

Ella Jones (Peggy), *pages 32–39, 162–63*. Home designed by Ella Jones and Magnus Pettersen.

Tania and Duncan McNab (Kiba), *pages 130–37*. Hepburn House in Kent.

Richard Nott and Graham Fraser (Albert and Raf), *pages 114–21*

Philip Oakley and Olivia Yip (Joe and Jarvis), *pages 102–109*

Marian and Richard Sanderson (Dougie), *pages 18–23*

Wayne and Adam Entwisle Shires (Sid and Pip), *pages 110–13*

Nikki Tibbles (Smith, Ronnie, Rita, Ruby, and Lenny), *pages 78–87, 168–73*

Peter and Sophia Willasey (Percy), *pages 96–101*

Mark Winwood (Flynn), *pages 24–31, 160–61*

Yvonne and Martin (Milo, Otis, and Hardy), *pages 146–55, 166–67*

ACKNOWLEDGMENTS

I would like to dedicate this book to my grandchildren Finlay and Marnie. I hope they get as much joy from dogs as their mother Rosie and I have.

Thank you to Cindy Richards, Sally Powell, Toni Kay, Penny Craig, and Carmel Edmonds from CICO Books for supporting me through the process of photographing, writing, and delivering this book.

Huge thanks to James Gardiner, the very skilled photographer who was generous with his time and patience. We completely disagree with the saying "Never work with animals," as the dogs were a real joy—especially if there was cheese at hand.

Thank you to all the dogs and dog owners, for allowing us into your beautiful homes to create what I think is a wonderful proof of how beautiful homes and dogs can go hand in hand. And thanks to Ian and Vanessa for help in finding the locations and dog owners.

Thanks also to all the dog rescue organizations who work so hard to reduce the suffering of dogs far and wide.

To my daughter Rosie, who is my biggest support, thank goodness your maternity leave fell during the making of this book.

And finally a big thank you to Eddie, my own dog, who has offered so much inspiration for this book.